THE FOUR ELEMENTS

Also By The Author:
_____

Last Resorts
Unscientific Americans
Parallel Universes
Poems and Songs
Mondo Boxo

THE FOUR ELEMENTS

cartoons by
Roz Chast

HARPER & ROW, PUBLISHERS,   New York
Cambridge, Philadelphia, San Francisco, London,
Mexico City, São Paulo, Singapore, Sydney

1817

For Bill and Ian

Of the 114 drawings in this collection, 78 originally appeared in The New Yorker. Copyright © 1984, 1985, 1986, 1987, 1988 by The New Yorker Magazine, Inc. Grateful acknowledgment is made to The New Yorker for permission to reprint.

Several cartoons have also appeared in Mother Jones and The Sciences.

FIRST EDITION

LIBRARY OF CONGRESS CATALOGUE CARD NUMBER: 88-45020

ISBN: 0-06-096294-1

88 89 90 91 92 HOR 10 9 8 7 6 5 4 3 2 1

PROFILES IN COURAGE

IT'S THE HIGHWAY FOR PEOPLE WHO HATE TO DRIVE

"All those trucks careening toward you at 90 m.p.h. — it makes me sick!"

"What if you get lost?"

"What if the steering wheel comes off in your hands?"

"I hate it — I just hate the whole idea of it!"

INTRODUCING THE

POKY LITTLE PARKWAY

This is great!

- 5 lanes in either direction: SLOW, REALLY SLOW, INCREDIBLY SLOW, CRAWL, and STANDSTILL
- Maximum speed — 25 m.p.h.
- Each lane is 40 ft. wide and separated from the one next to it by a 3 ft. wide "mistake aisle"
- Drivers are alerted to each exit WELL IN ADVANCE
- No trucks
- No passing

So buckle up, calm down, and HEAD FOR THE OPEN ROAD!

r. chat

CAT FADS
OF APARTMENT 11-N

For a while, anything "in creamy gravy" was the thing. Then suddenly, nothing but tuna would do.

The blue chair was big last month, but this month, it's the far right corner of the livingroom.

Finally, one wonders why the beloved dented ping pong ball of a week ago is now just so much dross

R. Chast

ON THE PLUS SIDE

WELCOME TO
ALASKA
PLENTY OF STORAGE SPACE FOR EVERY MAN, WOMAN, AND CHILD

Welcome to
IDAHO
HOME OF AMAZINGLY INEXPENSIVE 3-BEDROOM APARTMENTS

WELCOME TO
CENTRAL IOWA
A NICE PLACE TO LIVE
A FANTASTIC PLACE TO PARK

R. Chast

Dumbo's Distant Cousins

BIMBO

RUMBO

MAMBO

DIMBO

RAMBO

R. Chast

THE COLLECTOR'S CORNER

by Marvin Marvinview

Dear Marvin,

I happen to have in my possession three rubber bands, tan. 2½" long, in good condition. Are they worth anything?

R.K.,
Queens, N.Y.

Dear R.K.,

Those rubber bands will be worth a lot of money someday. Save 'em.

Marvin

Dear Marvin,

I keep saving rinsed-out jars from jams, jellies, ketchup, tomato sauce, etc. Lately, I've been wondering if it's time to give them the old heave-ho. What's your advice?

J.N.,
Cheyenne, Wyo.

Dear J.N.,

Don't you read this column? Haven't I always said, "Throw it away and hell you'll pay"?? What is with you ???

Marvin

Dear Marvin,

I have a whole bunch of keys in a drawer that don't go to anything. Could they be valuable?

S.P.,
Akron, Ohio

Dear S.P.,

Naturally they could be valuable, but not if you toss them out. Whatever you do, hang on to them.

Marvin

R. Chast

SEASONS AND THEIR BUDGETS

SPRING: New leaves; birds; flowers; rain; grass ~ $286,938,557,651,921,000.⁰⁰

FALL: Dyes for leaves ~ $109,692,280,553,281,000.⁰⁰

WINTER: Snow ~ $878,652,339,102,000.⁰⁰

SUMMER: More rain; grass; leaves ~ $486,229,357,293,000.⁰⁰

R. Chast

GUY WONDERS

Mr. B.J. ~ His rent actually equals his weekly salary.

Mr. L.R. ~ Returns the unused portions of things he's not satisfied with.

Mr. V.S. ~ Always answers the phone on the second ring

Hello?

R. Chast

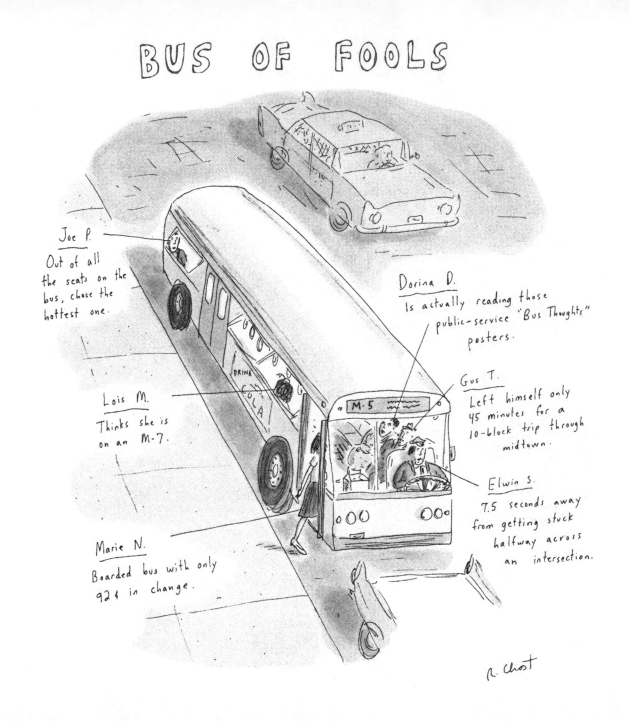

STORES OF MYSTERY

Fred's Drugs

Surrounded by cut-rate drug-and-cosmetic emporiums that sell, let's say, a bottle of XYZ shampoo for 79¢. Same bottle at Fred's? $2.09 !!! How does he do it?

Beauty-Moi Frocks

Weird clothes, always five seasons out of date. Has been there forever. Store is usually pretty empty except for racks and racks of pants suits and the like. Who shops here?

M & O Typewriter Supplies

This place has been closed whenever one has walked by it. However, it's *always* *there*, meaning somebody is continuing to pay rent on it. Why?

Tip-Top Goods

Boxes of saltines next to cartons of hair spray. Wigs. Christmas decorations, halter tops, institutional-sized jars of olives. Did all of this stuff "fall off a truck" or what?

r. Chast

For the Adventurous Only —
THE INWARD BOUND EXPERIENCE

Panel 1: You and six other people are locked in a 9' x 12' studio apartment for three weeks.

Panel 2: For food, you have only what is in the house, plus items from whatever restaurants will deliver.

"Anchovies, extra cheese. Thank you."

Panel 3: For entertainment, there is an old black-and-white TV, volume "G" of the World Book Encyclopedia, and each other. THAT IS ALL!

"So... what do you do?"

Panel 4: You will face many perils, like horrible neighbors.

BOOGIE 'TIL THE PLASTER CRACKS, UHN, UHN, UHN

Panel 5: You will form friendships that will last *your* entire lives.

Best wishes for a happy holiday season.
Bob Jones and Family

Panel 6: And when it's over, you'll be a changed person.

"The usual, Mr. Felton?"

"Guess again, Shirley!"

R. Chast

RADIATOR COOKERY

JUNK STAMPS FOR JUNK MAIL

r. Chast

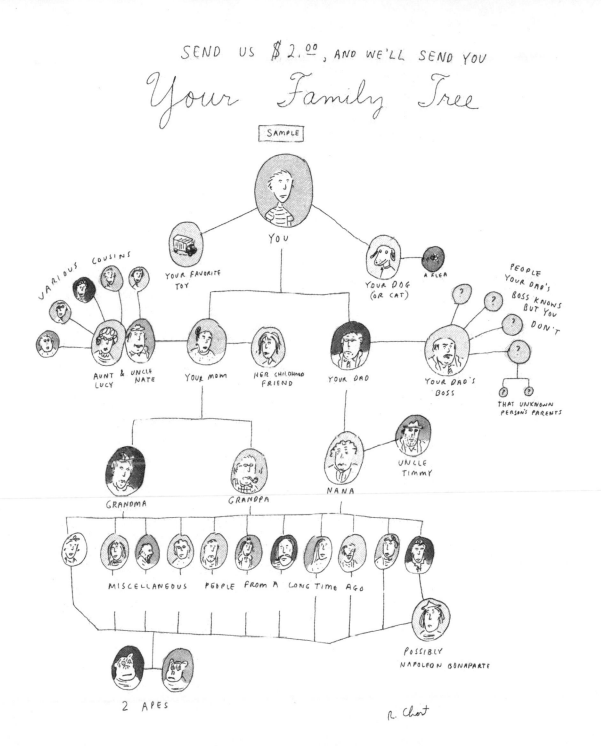

CONSUMERS' REVIEW

WITH HENRY TOTHERO

THIS WEEK: RUBBER BANDS

BRAND	COST	RATING	COMMENTS
Snappy Wonder®	$1.79 per 100	A –	Resilient and attractively packaged. Stretched to fit around Volumes A–E of the World Book Encyclopedia prior to breakage. Somewhat more expensive than most.
Drawer Pal®	.99 per 100	B+	Nice rubbery texture. Most bands expanded to fit around head before snapping.
Band-King®	.59 per 100	B –	Bands varied in quality from good to unacceptable. Depressing grey color.
Tan Expando®	.69 per 100	C –	Peculiar smell. Suspect use of low-grade, recycled rubber. Would use only if no other band was around.
Acme®	.29 per 100	F	The bottom of the barrel. Several bands in sample package were actually broken and then knotted!!!

r.Chast

SINGIN' IN THE RAIN

ROGUE SALAD BAR

KEYS · PENNIES · POCKET LINT · STAMPS · OIL · VINEGAR · SHOELACES · TISSUES · OLD NEGATIVES · BUTTONS · BOBBY PINS · CHECKERS

CORRECTION FLUIDS

For painters — KORRECT-O-KANVAS

For actors — OBLIT-O-SCENE

For everybody — LIFE-OUT

R. Chast

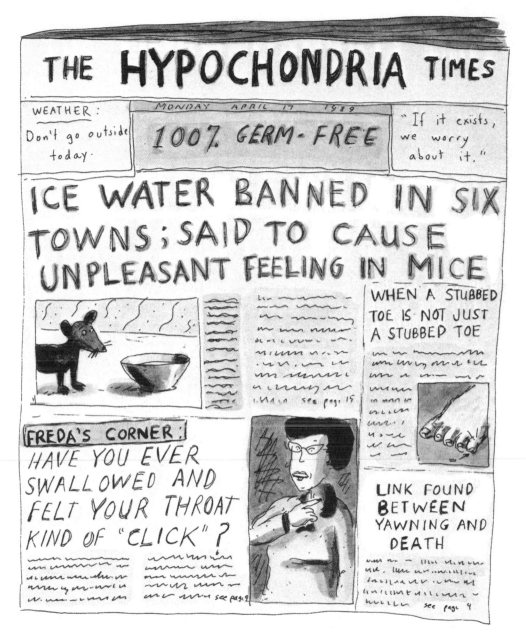

ROCK BOTTOM AMUSEMENT PARK

① Start your kids off with a visit to the "Run-Around-Like-a-Maniac" ride. For only 50¢, your child gets to run around like a maniac with anywhere between 1 and 100 other little tykes for 1 full hour.

② After that, they'll be so pooped that you can take them on the Bench to Nowhere. 75¢ buys ½ hour of excitement.

③ A big favorite of kids of all ages is a visit to the Man-Made Geyser, only $1.²⁵ per child.

④ The fun never stops, even when you leave.

R. Chast

THE THRILL IS GONE

Ball-point pens

Instant cake mixes

TV

COUNTRY-EASTERN MUSIC

"My Baby Took the N Train (and Didn't Look Back)"/ The Turnstylists

"Hard-Hearted Landlord"/ Rona and the Renters

"T-R-A-F-F-I-C"/ Wayne Gridlock

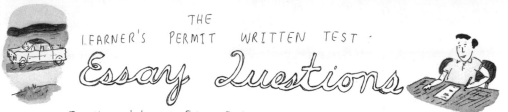

THE LEARNER'S PERMIT WRITTEN TEST ·
Essay Questions

1. In the style of Edna Ferber, contrast and compare thruway, freeway, highway, and turnpike.

2. Two authors approach an intersection at the same moment. One has eleven books under his belt (all of which did o.k.). The other has only one, but it was a _massive best seller_ as well as a _critical success_. Who has the right of way? Why?

3. A bus, a taxi, a stretch limousine, a Dodge Dart, and a Mercedes plow into each other on Broadway and 47th Street at rush hour. Write about the incident from the viewpoints of the drivers of each vehicle in each of their respective dialects.

4. Write a sonnet about parallel parking.

5. Choose three of the following signs and explain their metaphysical meanings in all of post-Freudian literature.

R. Chast

MUZAK'S TOP 10

1. Calm, Calm You
2. Fill Up Your Cart
3. Let's Wait in This Room Forever
4. Aisle Six Polka
5. (Don't Be Nervous 'Bout) Root Canal
6. Unnoticeable Sonata in B-flat
7. Please Don't Shoplift
8. Elevator Jamboree (Otis' Song)
9. Let's Buy Some More
10. Isn't Shopping Fun?

R. Chast

ODD SPAS

LA MAISON DU POULET

Guests must consume one small boiled chicken every day, bones and all. Cost: $7,500.⁰⁰ per week

FRIEDA'S REJUVENATION CENTER

2 glasses of black-cherry soda 8 times per day, plus a Milky Way just before bed. Cost: $10,000.⁰⁰ per week

THE HORIZON WORKSHOP

All the coffee and doughnuts you can eat. Cost: $15,000.⁰⁰ per week.

R. Chast

UNWISE INVESTMENTS

Stumblebum

SIRED BY: CLUMSY OAF
OUT OF: LADY UH-OH

Galloping Consumption

SIRED BY: MISTER PROUST
OUT OF: PENICILLIN

Molasses in January

SIRED BY: BUMP ON A LOG
OUT OF: JUST DOZING

R. Chast

THIS SUMMER, SPOIL YOURSELF SILLY WITH A...

POCKET BARBECUE!

Anytime!

Anywhere!

Suddenly, I had a craving!

Buy

r. Chast

GIFTS FOR CHILDREN*

* OTHER PEOPLE'S

All-Day Xylophone
Kids will adore this xylophone — they'll start playing it at 5:30 A.M. and won't stop until it's time for bed.....$12.⁹⁵

Robotman
Boys and girls are bound to have a lot of fun with Robotman. Needs only 80 batteries for a full 2 hours of excitement.

Artville Markers
Children love to draw everywhere and anywhere with these markers. Best of all, they're completely indelible.........$5.⁹⁵

r. Chast

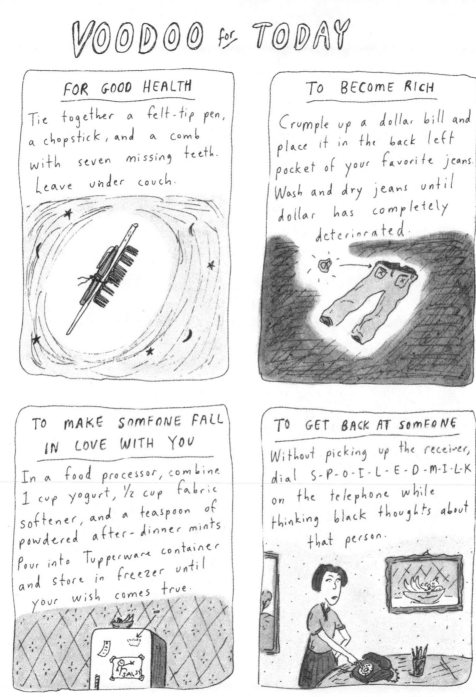

THE 1487 East 16th Street
BOOK CLUB

MAKE YOUR OWN

CHRISTMAS TREE
You'll need:
- An old broom
- Lots of imagination

ORNAMENTS
You'll need:
- Shredded wheat
- Plenty of nerve

GIFT WRAP
You'll need:
- Newspaper
- Excellent gifts

R. Chast

ED'S
ODD JOB LOT

END·OF·THE·DECADE
CLEARANCE [LAST 2 YEARS]

CHEESY STUDIO
APARTMENT CONDOS
in UGLY NEW
BUILDINGS
$13.99

BLUE MARGARITA
MIX 19¢

JAPANESE
HAUTE COUTURE
GARMENTS
49¢ per lb.

NOUVELLE
CUISINE
COOKBOOKS
2/79¢

AEROBICS
VIDEOTAPES
39¢

ADULT TRIVIA
GAMES
29¢

R. Chast

RECIPES FROM THE "I REALLY, REALLY HATE TO COOK" COOKBOOK

Lunchtime Surprise

6 old green olives
5/6 plum
3½ slices yellow American cheese
8 oyster crackers
bite of cheesecake
⅓ c. rice pudding
10 Necco wafers
Serves 1.

12 - Second Casserole

Throw a bunch of unspoiled stuff in a pot that won't blow up when you put it in the oven. Bake till hot.
Serves 1

Leftover Jamboree

Leftovers
Water

Do your best to find a clean pan. Heat food up with a little water. Serves 1

Ma Bell's Special

Takeout menu
Telephone

Decide what you're in the mood for. Dial. Order. Wait for delivery. Serves 1.

Chinese? ooo ooo Pizza?

R. Chast

TYROLEAN

Green shorts worn with suspenders by men	Certain alps	Yodeling	Meerschaum pipes

BORDERLINE TYROLEAN

Clogs	Obsession with owls, unicorns, etc.	Ice skating	Pre-packed cheese-and-sausage combos

NON·TYROLEAN

Maple trees	Conceptual art	Peanut-butter and jelly sandwiches	Thread

ANTI·TYROLEAN

The ocean   The color black   French couture, cuisine, and literature   Devil-may-care attitudes

R·Chast

IRREFUTABLE EVIDENCE

fragments of UFO that crash-landed last week near Lambert's Corner, Saskatchewan

Soil taken from site

Some photos taken just prior to landing of craft

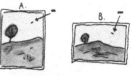

Enlarged photo (B.)

Drawings done by Mrs. Kitty Nederson, witness, while under hypnosis

Tape recording of nearby dog barking uncontrollably at time of visitation

R. Chast

MYRA'S LITTLE GARDEN

The corn was as low
As an elephant's toe.

R. Chast

FROM THE NOTEBOOK OF

Lewis Commonsense, Ph.D.

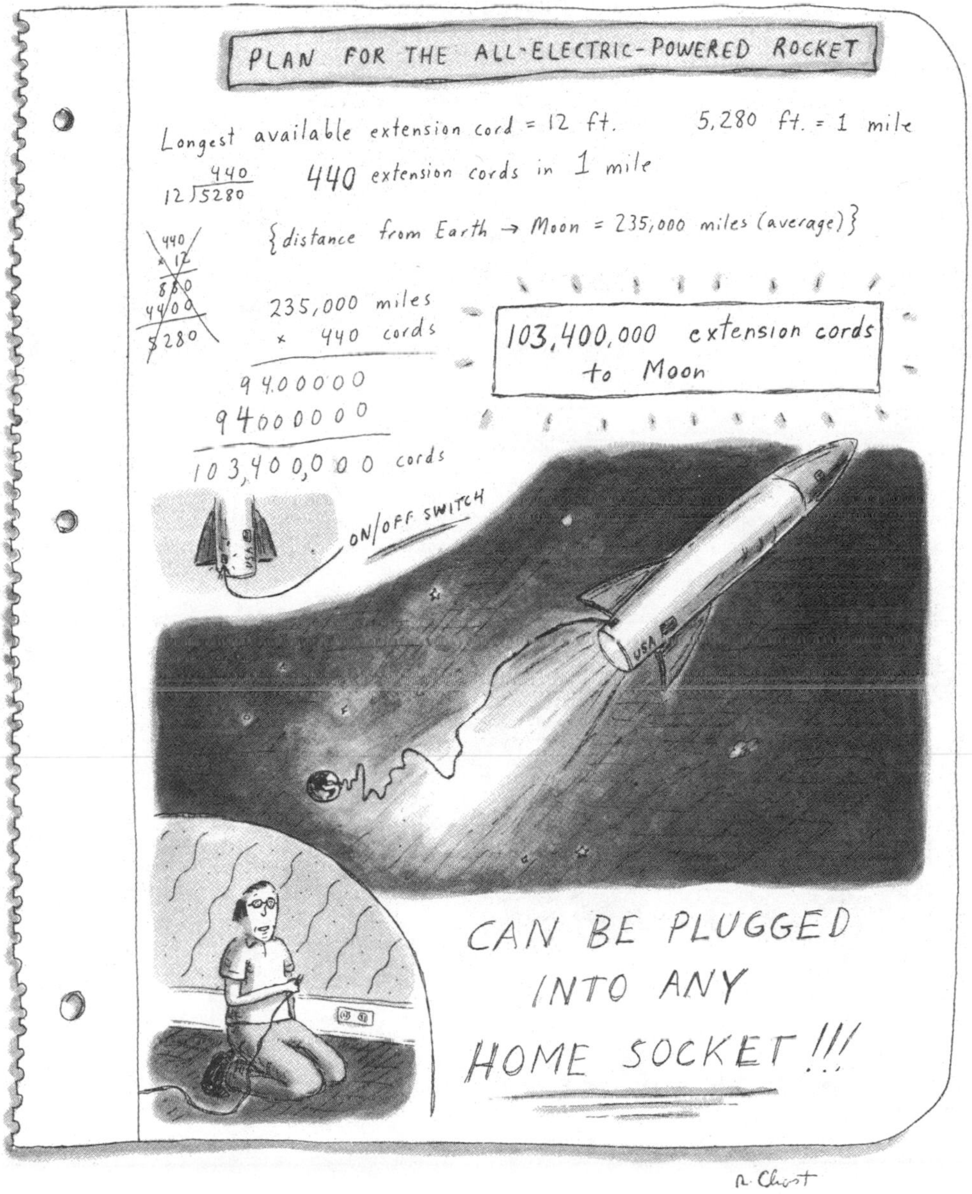

CLASSIFIEDS

PARKING SPOT for sale. West 79th Street, Manhattan. Must vacate this Sat. A.M. Box 927.

MIDTOWN REAL ESTATE – for building or farming Box 561.

GREAT VIEW – My apartment, your view. Come up as often as you like and look out window. By week or month. Box 834

R. Chast

POLLYANNA IN HELL

No more down jackets FOREVER!

Seems like a great place to hike!

Maybe I'll meet some neat people!

R. Chast

59¢
REAL
confessions
"I Can't Cook a Roast" by Betty Lo Elderson
"Driving Scares Me" by Joe Mahoney
"My Broker Turned Out to Be a Real Peabrain" by Alan Fields
"I Don't Care For Picasso" by Nancy Tremaine

R. Chast

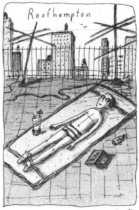

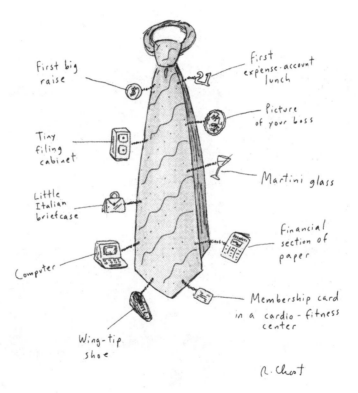

FOR THE SENTIMENTAL EXECUTIVE ~

THE CHARM TIE

First big raise

First expense-account lunch

Tiny filing cabinet

Picture of your boss

Martini glass

Little Italian briefcase

Financial section of paper

Computer

Membership card in a cardio-fitness center

Wing-tip shoe

R. Chast

THE ARRIVAL OF AUNT MATHILDA
Visit or Visitation?

Young Professional Recipe Test

FRIENDS OF THE FAMILY

CHILDREN'S PERSONALS

OVERLY SPECIFIC PRODUCTS

for the very specific kind of soil a _man_ gets on his clothes.

For shampooing your hair when you don't really need to - just when it's something to do.

Tastes great on first bite, but leaves awful aftertaste. For the rebellious pet.

Finally perfected: a remedy for the headache that stems from stuck car alarms.

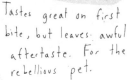

A floor wax of exceptional strength, concocted for those special occasions. She'll be able to see her face in your linoleum

R. Chast

They Never Caught On

R. Chast

REVISED TEXTS

Madame Bovary, Tennis Ace

Madame Bovary's mischief-creating boredom becomes a thing of the past when she discovers tennis.

The Great and Physically Fit Gatsby

The mystery man of West Egg changes his life by taking up running.

Hamlet, Swimmer of Denmark

The melancholy Prince learns that he can rid himself of anxiety and tension by swimming a mile a day.

R. Chast

FROM THE

DEPRESSING AISLE

Generic canned vegetables

Huge bags of off-brand candy

Waxed paper bags

Dietetic foods that relate more to illness than diets

Strange laundry products

Too many types of house slippers

R. Chast

LEARN TO BE A CRITIC IN THE PRIVACY OF YOUR OWN HOME, WITH THE

Apex Correspondence School of Criticism!

LESSON ONE - FREE OF CHARGE:

① If you want to say you liked somebody in a picture or whatever,
don't just say:

> So-and-So was pretty good, in my opinion, if I do say so myself.

Say:

> Move over, So-and-So, 'cause here comes SO-AND-SO!

> OR,

> So-and-So gives the performance of a lifetime!

② Here's another tip: If somebody asks you what you thought of something,
don't just say,

> Uh, I thought it was pretty good, I guess.

Say,

> I had a ROLLICKING GOOD TIME !!!

Interested? Write to: Apex Correspondence School of Criticism
Box 217-L
Lentils, Arizona

R. Chast

ANTIQUE DEALERS
OF
PERNMUT COUNTY

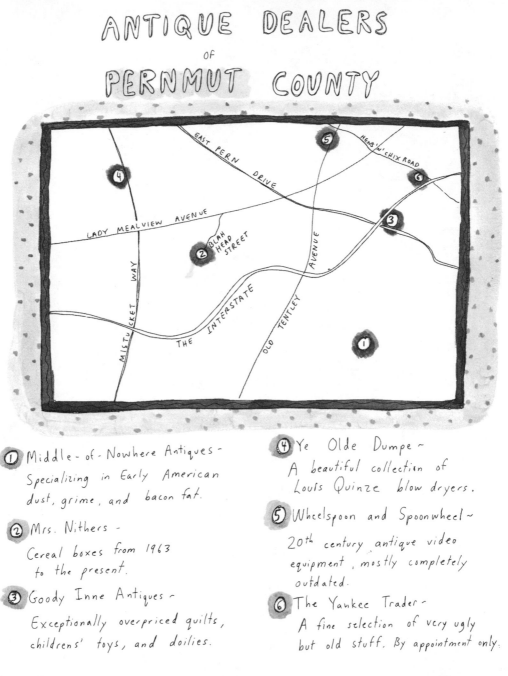

1. Middle-of-Nowhere Antiques - Specializing in Early American dust, grime, and bacon fat.

2. Mrs. Nithers - Cereal boxes from 1963 to the present.

3. Goody Inne Antiques - Exceptionally overpriced quilts, childrens' toys, and doilies.

4. Ye Olde Dumpe - A beautiful collection of Louis Quinze blow dryers.

5. Wheelspoon and Spoonwheel - 20th century antique video equipment, mostly completely outdated.

6. The Yankee Trader - A fine selection of very ugly but old stuff. By appointment only.

R. Chast

THE THREE WISE MEN OF GOTHAM

ERNIE ~ Is a total nitwit-bum, but gets invited to every single party all over town.

LARRY ~ Lives in an 18-room apartment on Central Park West. Rent? $167.²⁵

RAYMOND ~ Can make bus, train, or taxi show up merely by visualizing it.

R. Chast

For Him

Janitor-in-a-Flacon ~ The men's cologne with the distinct scent of ammonia.

JANITOR-IN-A-FLACON

Pool ~ The world's first turquoise-tinted, chlorine-based fragrance.

POOL

My Scotch ~ No one can resist the essence of whiskey on a man's neck.

my scotch

R. Chast

NON-CELEBRITY ROAST

Low-Rent Stockbrokers

The Follow-Up

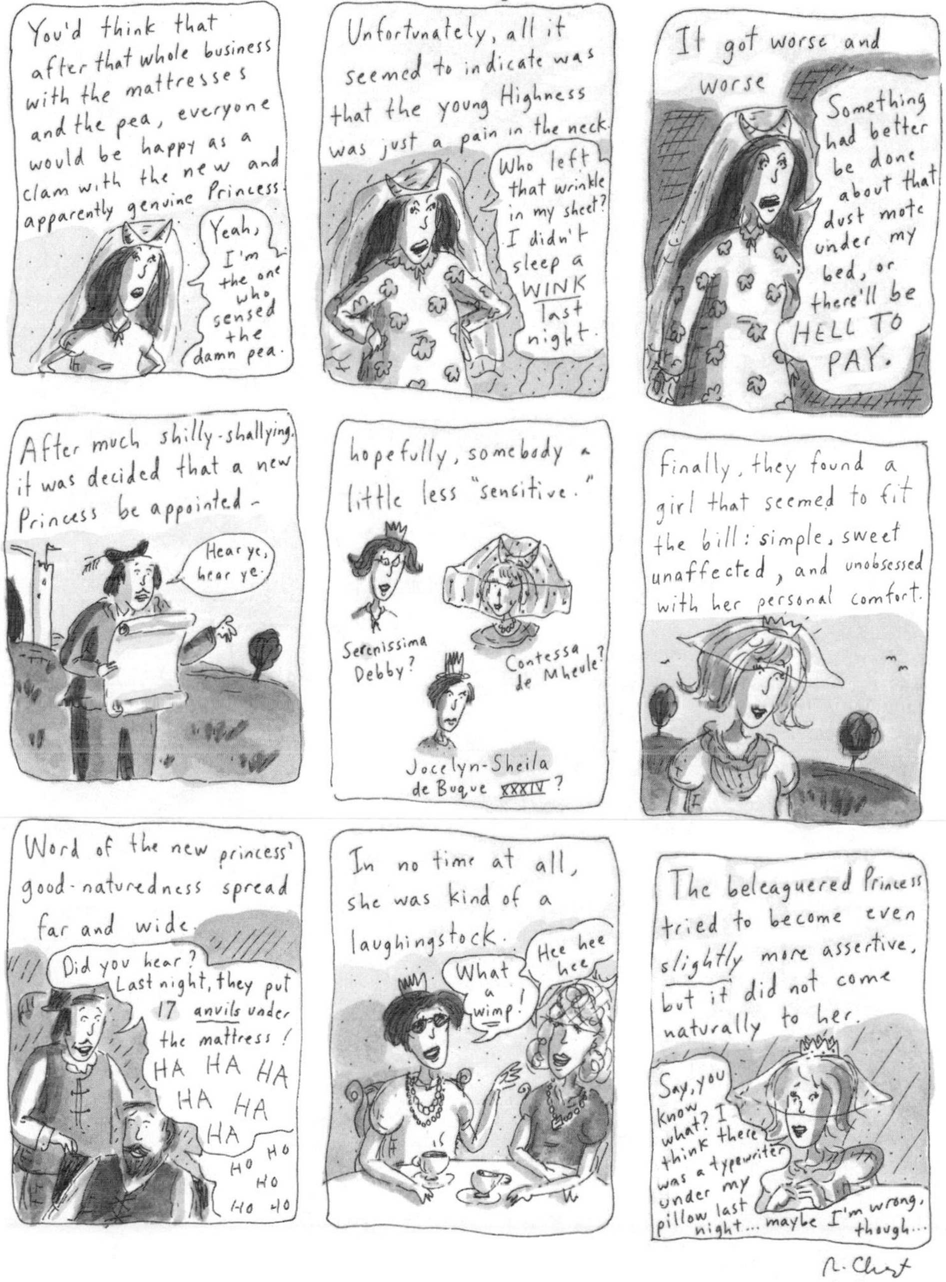

THE WORLD'S SILLIEST IDEAS

The _entire_ _universe_ could be inside the sandwich of some huge being about to have us for lunch!

There is no reason to doubt that all Heaven and Earth is squished into a piece of dust on the needle of a phonograph belonging to a large organism!

Life as we know it could be going on in a gigantic alien child's pencil case that fell behind a bookcase!

Our existence could be taking place inside of an immense wastepaper basket!

It is possible that everything in our cosmos is happening in an unimaginably colossal person's discarded hatbox!

What if our being was occurring in the space between the pen point and the cap on a pen in the jacket pocket of a very _very_, _very_ big humanoid?

R. Chast

DIARY OF A CAT

TODAY
Today I got some food in a bowl. It was great! I slept some, too

TODAY
Played with yarn. Got some food in a bowl. Had a good nap

TODAY
Slept. food, yarn. Fun!

TODAY
I played with a shoelace. Ate. slept. A good day.

TODAY
Slept Ate some food. Yum.

TODAY
Food in a bowl. Yarn galore Dozed for quite a while.

TODAY
Had a good nap. Then food in a bowl. Then yarn.

r. Chast

THE DARK SIDE OF AUTUMN

Chestnuts exploding in the oven.

BOOM KA-POW BLAMMO

Pumpkins going bad.

Parade balloons that didn't quite make the grade this year.

KIRBY KRICKET
BANJO BOB
CLOVER, THE WONDER HORSE

R. Chast

How Much Should You Tip?

SALESPEOPLE

10% of purchase price is adequate, but 15% is gracious

GRATUITIES

TEACHERS

20% of tuition at the end of the semester is the usual amount

POURBOIRES

LANDLORDS

25% of rent at Christmastime is deemed appropriate in most circles

TENANTS·59 EAST
ELM STREET

R. Chast

THE NERVOUS GOURMET

This week: **LOW-RISK CHICKEN**

1. Get or pay someone to light the oven for you
2. Place chicken in oven using six-foot tongs.
3. Bake it for 1-1½ hours while you are close enough to make sure that the heat from the oven isn't setting anything on fire, but far enough away so that if, by any chance, the oven should explode, you will escape with only minor injuries.
4. Make arrangements to have someone remove chicken from oven while you stand at the opposite end of the kitchen.
5. Put on oven mitt and turn off oven.

YOUR FRIEND

Next week: **TOAST WITHOUT ANXIETY**

r. Chast

THE
JUKES
AND THE
KALLIKAKS
TODAY

Ed Jukes –
prominent real-estate developer

Amanda Kallikak –
attorney for Pastoral Nuclear
Waste Manufacturers Inc.

Lance Kallikak –
hot young graffiti artist

Judy Ann Jukes –
newest queen of workout videos

R. Chast

DISTRACTIONS OF THE GREAT

Here's Jane Austen. She's supposed to be writing, but she's getting her hair cut in _two hours_!

And Verdi. He's got an opera due in *three weeks*! But what about that chocolate cake in the pantry?

Henri Matisse was not at all immune, especially when it came to cats.

Why, this even happened to Madame Curie.

R. Chast

A TREND REVIVED

Club Soda Bed~ Just don't overfill it or move it around too violently.

KABOOMBA

Brie Bed~ Very comfortable, especially at room temperature. Must be set up in a well-ventilated area, however.

Flan Bed~ Good consistency, but filling tends to "disappear" after a week or two

R. Chast

SUPPLEMENTARY SCARLET LETTERS

Non-Jogger

NJ

Poor Credit Risk

PCR

Computer Illiterate

C I

R. Chast

MINI·REBELLIONS

WHAT CITIES COULD BUY IF EVERY SINGLE INHABITANT CONTRIBUTED JUST <u>ONE</u> <u>MEASLY</u> <u>DOLLAR</u> TOWARD AN APARTMENT IN GLAMOROUS NEW YORK CITY

Convenient for when somebody comes to town!

Good place for parties!

My sister's town did it last year!

Great investment!

It's only a dollar apiece! C'mon!!

You'll feel good about yourself!

CITY	POPULATION	WHAT COULD BUY
AKRON, OHIO	237,177	Charming 1 bdrm. walkup, no light, no closets, low 90s, East Side.
SPOKANE, WASHINGTON	171,300	Lovely mini-loft, above rubber-band factory, right in the heart of SoHo.
TOPEKA, KANSAS	115,266	Delightful studio, can be converted into 2 bdrms. West 150s.
MUNCIE, INDIANA	77,216	Studio, over 80 sq. ft., Queens.
IDAHO FALLS, IDAHO	39,590	Nothing

R. Chast

LLOYD:

A MAN WHO WOULDN'T KNOW A GOOD TIME IF IT HIT HIM ON THE HEAD, KNOCKED HIM OUT COLD, TIED HIS HANDS AND FEET, AND LEFT HIM IN A LITTLE TOOL SHED TO PERISH.

R. Chast

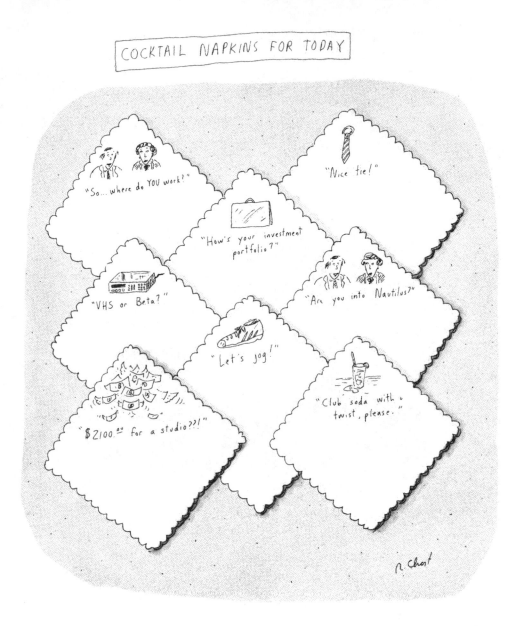

R. Chast

NEW **GIRL SCOUT** BADGES

 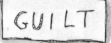 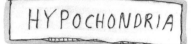

Can be earned by completing 4 hours of each of the following:

1) Rearranging a drawer
2) Reading any old thing that happens to be lying around; e.g., volume "B" of an encyclopedia; a computer magazine; a pamphlet of carrot recipe
3) Recopying an address

This badge is given to every Girl Scout who has spent 12 hours picking apart something that doesn't matter at all to anyone in this world or the next.

A badge specially designed for the Girl Scout who has spent 6 hours reading about fatal, horrible diseases and another 6 sure that she is suffering from one.

R. Chast

NEW I.R.S. GUIDELINES

All bath toys are deductible.

Children with less than a
B average are no longer deductible.

Mortgage payments made on houses
not <u>completely</u> encased in aluminum
siding are not deductible.

Three cats count as one dependent.

If somebody steps on your
toe and then gives you $1.00,
you must declare it.

For every glass of buttermilk
consumed during the fiscal
year, deduct $1.50.

R. Chast

SIDESHOW
OF THE FUTURE

SEE THE
WOMAN WITHOUT A B.A.!

GAZE FREELY AT THE
Last Guy Who Doesn't Have an Answering Machine!

★ LOOK UPON THE ★
ONLY FAMILY IN **AMERICA** THAT HAS NEVER MADE A TRIP TO A SALAD BAR!

R. Chast

GAMES TO PLAY WITH KIDS
IN THE CAR

"Churchmouse" ~ First one who makes the slightest peep loses.

"Telepathy" ~ Everybody tries to send their thoughts to everybody else without speaking.

"Foxhole" ~ Children pretend that they are in a foxhole on a battlefield and therefore must not utter a sound.

R. Chast

SECOND-HAND CHARACTERS

Fully formed, just like new. Cut from novel at last minute. Good as schoolmarm, nanny, etc. Contact Box 193.

Writer's block? No time? Just plain lazy? Whole family must go: Aristocratic, Southern, alcoholic, well-thought-out. Halfway through book, got cold feet. Box 495.

Extremely true-to-life selfish yet innocent guy needs to learn some tough lessons about life. Author too close, doesn't have the heart. Box 672.

R. Chast

PLEASE DON'T DROP DEAD DRESSES

Harmless ensemble of pale beige.

Are you sure?

Nothing is amiss in this tasteful ecru-tinted garment.

I hope you like it.

As mild and pleasant as a lukewarm glass of milk.

You don't think it's just a little MUCH?

R. Chast

New On The Scene

Your Mother's Moustache

Early 20th century decor. Drinks with names like "Trolley Car" and "Model-T." Peanuts served in Keystone Kop helmets. Ten organ grinders and their monkeys provide continuous entertainment.

Hoppity's

Women aren't left out at Hoppity's where peppy guys 'n' gals alike don rabbit costumes to serve patrons. If getting really embarrassed is your idea of a good time, then this is the place for you.

Schopenhauer's Retreat

Walls painted black. Sad German music on jukebox. Uncomfortable chairs; warm, flat, beer; and extremely stale popcorn not served in any kind of container, just thrown on each rickety table.

R. Chast.

Come see brawny Akitas pull many times their weight in Sunday papers!

Admire prize-winning produce culled by entrants from Korean markets throughout the 5-borough area!

Up on Machinery Hill, you'll be able to inspect state-of-the-art food processors, pasta makers, and VCR equipment!

And visit the numerous "All-You-Can-Eat-of-French-Haute-Cuisine" stands—they're *always* a big hit!

Dinner at the Mortgage Restaurant

Ever seen a meal you fell in love with but simply couldn't afford?

Well, at the Mortgage Restaurant you can afford just about anything.

THE MORTGAGE

Every table comes with not only a waiter but an accountant and a lawyer, all of whom would love to be of service.

Here's how it works: Let's say you want the baby lamb chops with baby potatoes and baby vegetables listed on our menu for $185.00.

For as little as $18.50 you can have that meal brought right to your table.

And in only 20 years you can call it your own.

R. Chast

TOTAL LOSS PICTURES.®

presents:

FORBIDDEN QUESTIONS

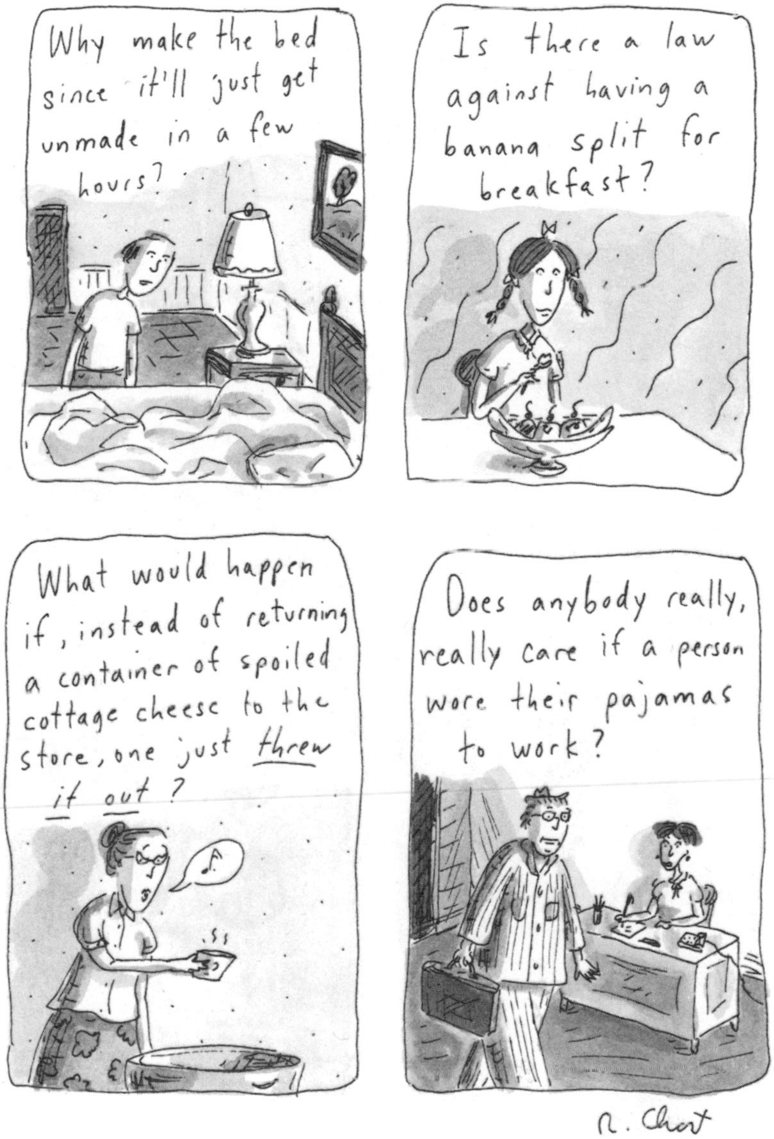

GET-WELL CARDS
for
UNDER-THE-WEATHER APPLIANCES

GET WELL SOON!

Contrast's gone?
Picture shot?
Don't know what it is
you've got?
You'll soon be fixed,
but even so
We miss your cheerful
little glow.

IN THE SHOP?

Cold blows warm,
Hot blows cold.
Fact is, friend,
you're getting old.
HOPE YOU'RE
REPAIRED SOON.

TO A SICK DRYER...

You burned a shirt,
You charred the socks,
You gave the folks electric
shocks.
A leaky hose, a missing screw,
We hope that's all that's
wrong with you.

R. Chast

SOCIAL CONTRACTS

Bob will not step on Joe's toe simply because it has crossed his mind to do so.

Mary will not set Betty Lou's hair afire even if it really gets on her nerves.

Tom will not plow his car through the Bakers' house although they deserve it.

R. Chast

IT'S TIME FOR <u>YOU</u> TO START BANKING AT THE

FIRST NATIONAL ARTISTE SAVINGS & LOAN

Friendly tellers who will never, <u>ever</u> laugh at you.

Special loans having nothing to do with real estate or cars.

Interesting, unbourgeois premiums.

Signed Dali lithograph (unframed)

Recently reissued Ornette Coleman record

Paperback of Walt Whitman's poems

Officers who understand your particular set of problems.

R. Chast

WHAT WENT WRONG?
Never owned dog?
Had strange middle name?
Johnny Xerxes Miller
Did not learn to play a musical instrument?
Too much fruit salad in early life?
R. Chast

THINGS *NOT* TO TELL YOUR KID

Sometimes we drink milk from cows and sometimes we drink milk from horses like the ones in Central Park.

There's a big stopper at the bottom of the ocean, and every once in a while it gets accidentally pulled out.

"The Wizard of Oz" is a true story.

Isn't this FUN?

Anything electrical can suddenly BLOW UP for no reason whatsoever.

TICK
TICK
TICK
TICK

r. Chast